A+ books

Bilingual Picture Dictionaries

My First Book of
Greek
Words

by Katy R. Kudela

Translator: Translations.com

apple
μήλο
(ME-lo)

CAPSTONE PRESS
a capstone imprint

Table of Contents

How to Use This Dictionary

This book is full of useful words in both Greek and English. The English word appears first, followed by the Greek word. Look below each Greek word for help to sound it out. Try reading the words aloud.

Topic Heading in English

Topic Heading in Greek

Word in English
Word in Greek
(pronunciation)

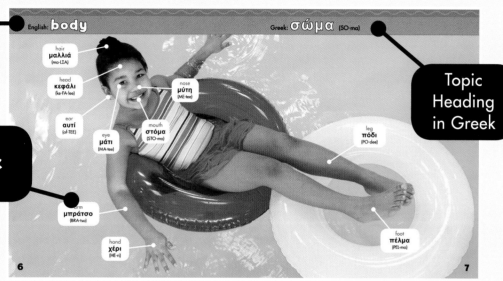

English: **body**

Greek: σῶμα (SO-ma)

hair
μαλλιά
(ma-LIA)

head
κεφάλι
(ke-FA-lee)

nose
μύτη
(ME-tee)

ear
αυτί
(af-TEE)

eye
μάτι
(MA-tee)

mouth
στόμα
(STO-ma)

leg
πόδι
(PO-dee)

arm
μπράτσο
(BRA-tso)

hand
χέρι
(HE-ri)

foot
πέλμα
(PEL-ma)

6

7

Notes about the Greek Language

The Greek alphabet has 24 letters. It is the oldest alphabet still in use.

The Greek language uses accents shown with a '. The accent means that your voice should stress the vowel with the accent.

There are sounds that do not exist in Greek. These sounds include:
[sh] as in "shop"   [z] as in "pleasure"   [ch] as in "church"

Most of the Greek letter prounuciations have sounds that are like English. To read the Greek characters, look at the pronunciation.

uncle
θείος
(THE-os)

mother
μητέρα
(mee-TE-ra)

cousin
εξάδελφος
(e-KSA-del-fos)

aunt
θεία
(THE-a)

baby
μωρό
(mo-RO)

grandmother
γιαγιά
(gia-GIA)

father
πατέρας
(pa-TE-ras)

grandfather
παππούς
(pa-POUS)

brother
αδερφός
(a-der-FOS)

sister
αδερφή
(a-der-FEE)

5

hair
μαλλιά
(ma-LIA)

head
κεφάλι
(ke-FA-lee)

nose
μύτη
(ME-tee)

ear
αυτί
(af-TEE)

mouth
στόμα
(STO-ma)

eye
μάτι
(MA-tee)

arm
μπράτσο
(BRA-tso)

hand
χέρι
(HE-ri)

leg
πόδι
(PO-dee)

foot
πέλμα
(PEL-ma)

pajamas
πυτζάμα
(pi-JA-ma)

coat
παλτό
(pal-TO)

shorts
σορτσάκι
(sor-TSA-kee)

boot
μπότα
(BO-ta)

shoe
παπούτσι
(pa-POO-tsee)

hat
καπέλο
(ka-PE-lo)

pants
παντελόνι
(pan-te-LO-nee)

sock
κάλτσα
(KAL-tsa)

dress
φόρεμα
(FO-re-ma)

shirt
πουκάμισο
(poo-KA-mee-so)

kite
χαρταετός
(har-ta-e-TOS)

doll
κούκλα
(KOO-kla)

puzzle
παζλ
(pazl)

train
τρένο
(TRE-no)

wagon
βαγόνι
(va-GO-nee)

puppet
μαριονέτα
(ma-rio-NE-ta)

skateboard
σκέιτμπορντ
(skate-board)

jump rope
σχοινάκι
(shee-NA-kee)

ball
μπάλα
(BA-la)

bat
μπαστούνι
(ba-STOU-nee)

window
παράθυρο
(pa-RA-thee-ro)

picture
φωτογραφία
(fo-to-gra-FI-a)

lamp
λάμπα
(LA-mpa)

dresser
ντουλάπι
(doo-LA-pee)

curtain
κουρτίνα
(koor-TI-na)

blanket
κουβέρτα
(ku-VER-ta)

door
πόρτα
(POR-ta)

pillow
μαξιλάρι
(ma-xi-LA-ri)

bed
κρεβάτι
(kre-VA-ti)

rug
χαλάκι
(ha-LA-kee)

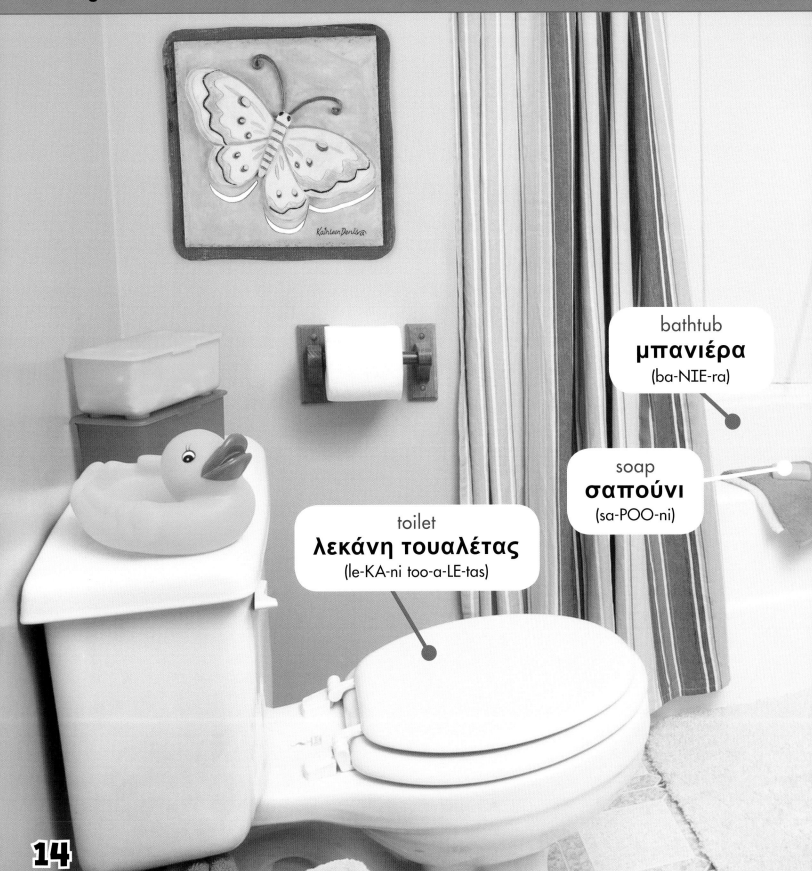

bathtub
μπανιέρα
(ba-NIE-ra)

soap
σαπούνι
(sa-POO-ni)

toilet
λεκάνη τουαλέτας
(le-KA-ni too-a-LE-tas)

mirror
καθρέφτης
(ka-THRE-ftis)

toothbrush
οδοντόβουρτσα
(o-do-DO-voor-tsa)

toothpaste
οδοντόκρεμα
(o-do-DO-kre-ma)

comb
χτένα
(HTE-na)

sink
νιπτήρας
(ne-ro-HE-tis)

towel
πετσέτα
(pe-TSE-ta)

brush
βούρτσα
(VOOR-tsa)

15

pot
κατσαρόλα
(ka-tsa-RO-la)

stove
εστία
(e-STI-a)

bowl
μπολ
(bol)

oven
φούρνος
(FOOR-nos)

refrigerator
ψυγείο
(psee-GEE-o)

knife
μαχαίρι
(ma-HE-ri)

spoon
κουτάλι
(koo-TA-lee)

plate
πιάτο
(PIA-to)

table
τραπέζι
(tra-PE-zi)

fork
πιρούνι
(pi-ROO-nee)

17

milk
γάλα
(GA-la)

carrot
καρότο
(ka-RO-to)

bread
ψωμί
(pso-MI)

apple
μήλο
(ME-lo)

butter
βούτυρο
(VU-tee-ro)

egg
αβγό
(av-GO)

pea
μπιζέλι
(bee-ZE-lee)

orange
πορτοκάλι
(por-to-KA-li)

sandwich
σάντουιτς
(SAN-toueets)

rice
ρύζι
(RE-zee)

tractor
τρακτέρ
(tra-KTER)

hay
σανός
(sa-NOS)

fence
φράχτης
(FRA-htees)

farmer
αγρότης
(a-GRO-tees)

sheep
πρόβατο
(PRO-va-to)

pig
γουρούνι
(gu-RU-nee)

20

horse
άλογο
(A-lo-go)

barn
αχυρώνας
(a-hee-RO-nas)

cow
αγελάδα
(a-ge-LA-da)

chicken
κοτόπουλο
(ko-TO-poo-lo)

21

leaf
φύλλο
(FE-lo)

butterfly
πεταλούδα
(pe-ta-LOO-da)

flower
λουλούδι
(lu-LU-dee)

shovel
φτυάρι
(FTIA-ree)

bird
πουλί
(pu-LE)

worm
σκουλήκι
(sku-LE-kee)

22

plant
φυτό
(fee-TO)

grass
γρασίδι
(gra-SE-dee)

dirt
βρωμιά
(vro-MIA)

seed
σπόρος
(SPO-ros)

23

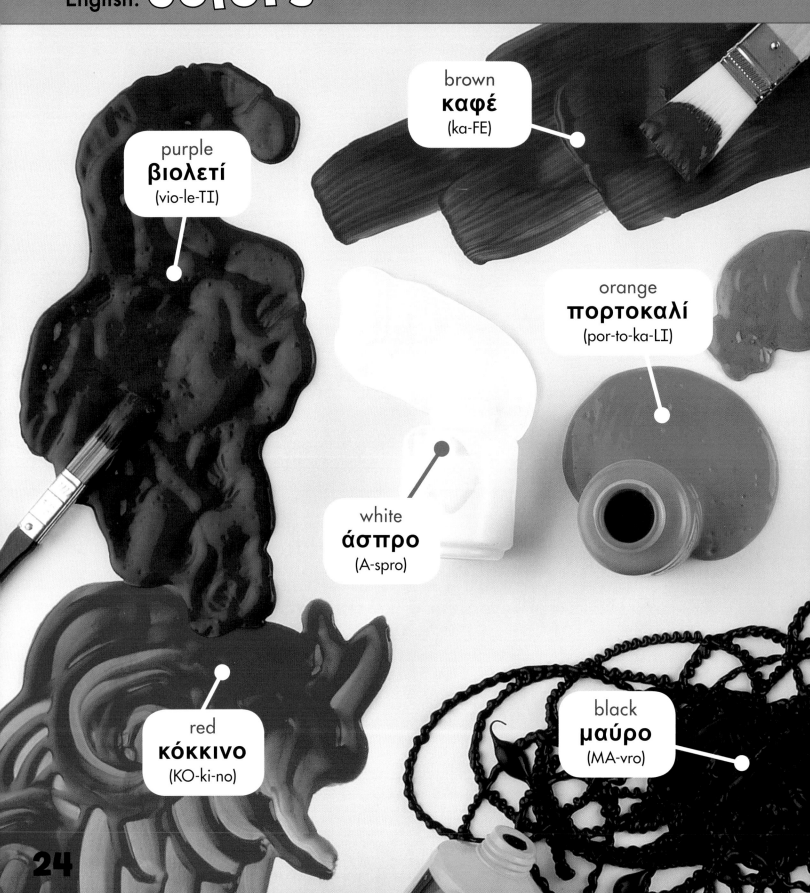

brown
καφέ
(ka-FE)

purple
βιολετί
(vio-le-TI)

orange
πορτοκαλί
(por-to-ka-LI)

white
άσπρο
(A-spro)

red
κόκκινο
(KO-ki-no)

black
μαύρο
(MA-vro)

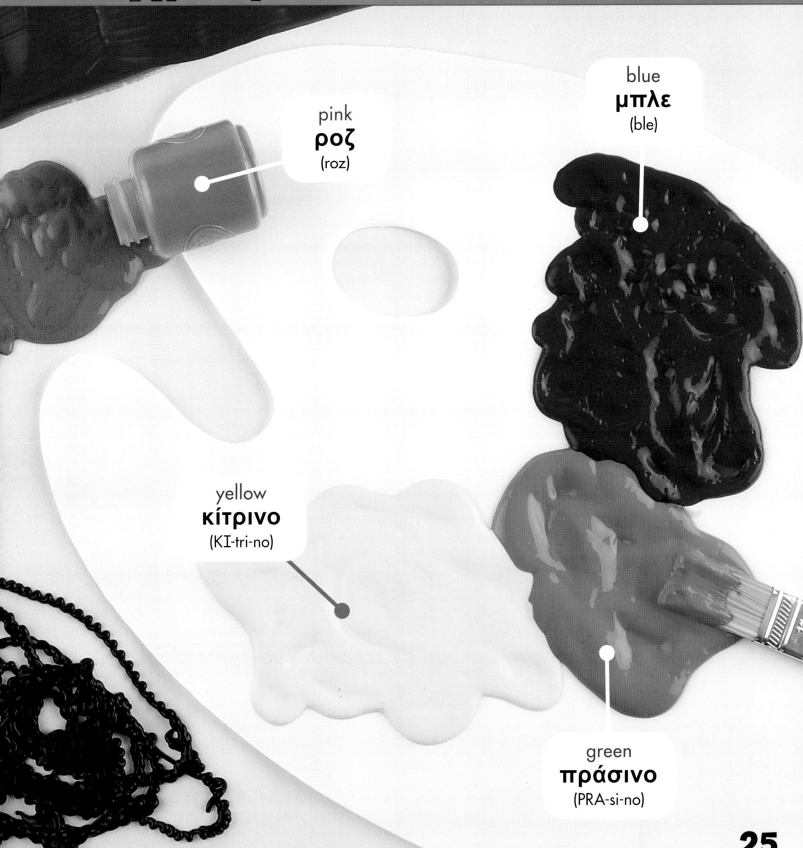

pink
ροζ
(roz)

blue
μπλε
(ble)

yellow
κίτρινο
(KI-tri-no)

green
πράσινο
(PRA-si-no)

teacher
δασκάλα
(da-SKA-la)

book
βιβλίο
(vi-VLI-o)

desk
γραφείο
(gra-FE-o)

pencil
μολύβι
(mo-LE-vi)

crayon
κραγιόνι
(kra-GIO-ni)

clock
ρολόι
(ro-LO-ee)

map
χάρτης
(HAR-tis)

computer
υπολογιστής
(ee-po-lo-gi-STIS)

chair
καρέκλα
(ka-RE-kla)

paper
χαρτί
(har-TE)

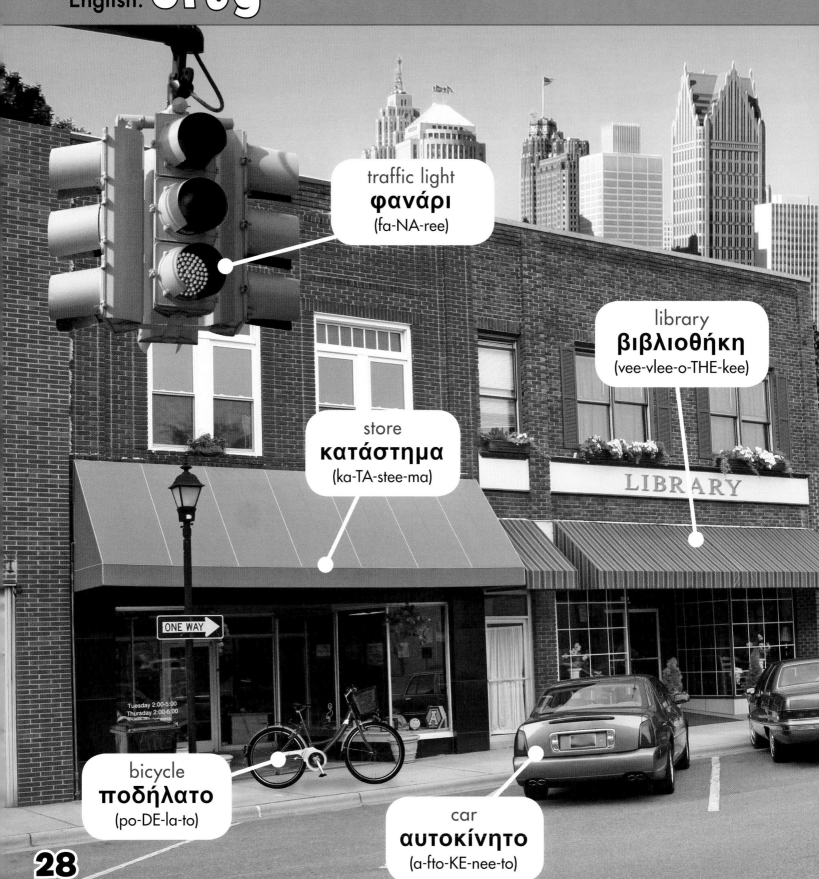

traffic light
φανάρι
(fa-NA-ree)

library
βιβλιοθήκη
(vee-vlee-o-THE-kee)

store
κατάστημα
(ka-TA-stee-ma)

LIBRARY

ONE WAY

Tuesday 2:00-5:00
Thursday 2:00-6:00

bicycle
ποδήλατο
(po-DE-la-to)

car
αυτοκίνητο
(a-fto-KE-nee-to)

Greek: **πόλη** (PO-lee)

tree
δέντρο
(DE-ntro)

bus
λεωφορείο
(le-o-fo-REE-o)

park
πάρκο
(PAR-ko)

street
δρόμος
(DRO-mos)

sign
πινακίδα
(pee-na-KE-da)

STOP

29

Numbers • Αριθμοί (a-rith-MOI)

1. one • **ένα** (E-na)
2. two • **δύο** (DI-o)
3. three • **τρία** (TRI-a)
4. four • **τέσσερα** (TE-se-ra)
5. five • **πέντε** (PE-nte)
6. six • **έξι** (E-ksi)
7. seven • **εφτά** (e-FTA)
8. eight • **οχτώ** (o-HTO)
9. nine • **εννιά** (e-NIA)
10. ten • **δέκα** (DE-ka)

Useful Phrases • Χρήσιμες φράσεις (HRI-si-mes FRA-sis)

yes • **ναι** (ne)

no • **όχι** (O-hi)

hello • **γεια** (GEIA-sou)

good-bye • **αντίο** (a-DI-o)

good morning • **καλημέρα** (ka-li-ME-ra)

good night • **καληνύχτα** (ka-li-NI-hta)

please • **παρακαλώ** (pa-ra-ka-LO)

thank you • **ευχαριστώ** (ef-ha-ri-STO)

excuse me • **με συγχωρείτε** (me seen-ho-REE-te)

My name is _____. • **Με λένε _____.** (me LE-ne)

Read More

Marsh, Carole. *It Really Is Greek to Me!: Greek for Kids.* Peachtree City, Ga.: Gallopade International, 2004.

Papaloizos, Theodore C. *My First Book.* Silver Spring, Md: Papaloizos Publications, 2007.

Internet Sites

FactHound offers a safe, fun way to find Internet sites related to this book. All of the sites on FactHound have been researched by our staff.

Here's all you do:

Visit www.facthound.com

Type in this code: 9781429596666

Super-cool stuff!

Check out projects, games and lots more at
www.capstonekids.com

A+ Books are published by Capstone Press,
1710 Roe Crest Drive, North Mankato, Minnesota 56003.
www.capstonepub.com

Books published by Capstone Press are manufactured with paper
containing at least 10 percent post-consumer waste.

Library of Congress Cataloging-in-Publication Data
Kudela, Katy R.
    My first book of Greek words / by Katy R. Kudela.
    p. cm. — (A+ Books, Bilingual picture dictionaries)
    Includes bibliographical references.
    Summary: "Simple text paired with themed photos invite the reader to learn to speak Greek"—
Provided by publisher.
    ISBN 978-1-4296-5966-6 (library binding)
    ISBN 978-1-4296-6171-3 (paperback)
    1. Picture dictionaries, Greek (Modern) 2. Picture dictionaries, English. 3. Greek language,
Modern.—Dictionaries, Juvenile—English. 4. English language—Dictionaries, Juvenile—Greek language,
Modern. I. Title.
PA1139.E5K83 2011
489'.3321—dc22   2010029468

Credits

Lori Bye, book designer; Wanda Winch, media researcher; Eric Manske, production specialist

Photo Credits

Capstone Studio/Gary Sundermeyer, cover (pig), 20 (farmer with tractor, pig)
Capstone Studio/Karon Dubke, cover (ball, sock), 1, 3, 4–5, 6–7, 8–9, 10–11, 12–13, 14–15,
    16–17, 18–19, 22–23, 24–25, 26–27
Image Farm, back cover, 1, 2, 31, 32 (design elements)
iStockphoto/Andrew Gentry, 28 (main street)
Photodisc, cover (flower)
Shutterstock/Adrian Matthiassen, cover (butterfly); David Hughes, 20 (hay); Eric Isselee,
    20–21 (horse); hamurishi, 28 (bike); Ievgeniia Tikhonova, 21 (chickens); Jim Mills, 29
    (stop sign); Kelli Westfal, 28 (traffic light); Margo Harrison, 20 (sheep); MaxPhoto, 21
    (cow and calf); Melinda Fawver, 29 (bus); Robert Elias, 20–21 (barn, fence); Vladimir
    Mucibabic, 28–29 (city skyline)

Note to Parents, Teachers, and Librarians
Learning to speak a second language at a young age has been shown to improve overall
academic performance, boost problem-solving ability, and foster an appreciation for other
cultures. Early exposure to language skills provides a strong foundation for other subject
areas, including math and reasoning. Introducing children to a second language can help
to lay the groundwork for future academic success and cultural awareness.

Printed in the United States of America in North Mankato, Minnesota.
112016   010148R